Federal Court Basics

The Structure and Function of Federal and State Courts

The Administrative Office of the United States Courts

Federal Court Basics

Master the structure and function of federal and state courts

Why Two Court Systems?

The Judicial Branch has two court systems: federal and state. While each hears certain types of cases, neither is completely independent of the other. The two systems often interact and share the goal of fairly handling legal issues.

The U.S. Constitution created a governmental structure known as federalism that calls for the sharing of powers between the national and state governments. The Constitution gives certain powers to the federal government and reserves the rest for the states.

The federal court system deals with legal issues expressly or implicitly granted to it by the U.S. Constitution. The state court systems deal with their respective state constitutions and the legal issues that the U.S. Constitution did not give to the federal government or explicitly deny to the states.

For example, because the Constitution gives Congress sole authority to make uniform laws concerning bankruptcies, a state court would lack jurisdiction. Likewise, since the Constitution does not give the federal government authority in most family law matters, a federal court would lack jurisdiction in a divorce case.

The federal judiciary is one of three equal but distinct branches of the federal government.

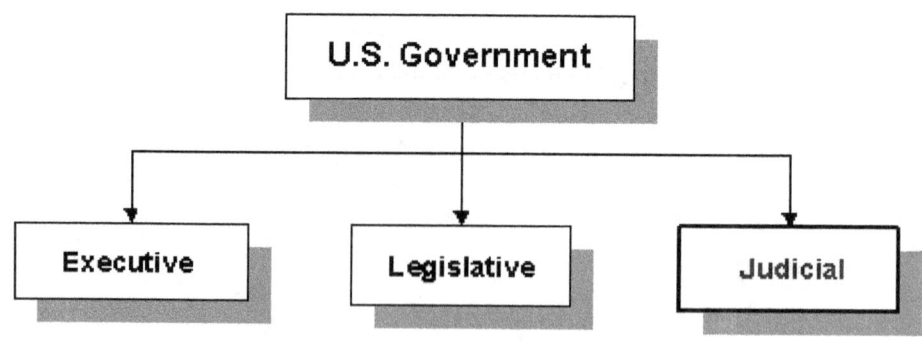

The framers of the Constitution created three equal branches to prevent any one branch from having too much power. Our country's system of government rests on a separation of powers. The legislative branch--Congress--makes the laws. The President and other executive branch departments execute and enforce the laws. It is the job of the judicial branch to apply and interpret the laws and to resolve disputes that arise under them. No branch may perform functions reserved for the other branches. Federal courts may exercise only judicial powers and perform only judicial functions, and judges may decide only cases that are before them.

The Constitution also creates a system of "checks and balances" among the three branches of government. This means that each branch has some powers over the other branches. For example, the President can veto legislation passed by Congress, which can, in turn, override the veto. The President appoints most federal judges, but the Senate must approve them. The courts interpret the laws that Congress enacts and may declare them unconstitutional.

The three branches of the federal government — legislative, executive, and judicial — operate within a constitutional system known as "checks and balances." This means that although each branch is formally separate from the other two, the Constitution often requires cooperation among the branches. Federal laws, for example, are passed by Congress and signed by the President. The judicial branch, in turn, has the authority to decide the constitutionality of federal laws and resolve other disputes over them, but judges depend upon the executive branch to enforce court decisions.

Federal Courts & Congress

The Constitution gives Congress the power to create federal courts other than the Supreme Court and to determine their jurisdiction. It is Congress, not the judiciary, that controls the type of cases that may be addressed in the federal courts.

Congress has three other basic responsibilities that determine how the courts will operate. First, it decides how many judges there should be and where they will work. Second, through the confirmation process, Congress determines which of the President's judicial nominees ultimately become federal judges. Third, Congress approves the federal courts' budget and appropriates money for the judiciary to operate. The judiciary's budget is a very small part — substantially less than one percent — of the entire federal budget.

Federal Courts & the Executive Branch

Under the Constitution, the President appoints federal judges with the "advice and consent" of the Senate. The President usually consults senators or other elected officials concerning candidates for vacancies on the federal courts. The President's power to appoint new federal judges is not the judiciary's only interaction with the executive branch. The Department of Justice, which is responsible for prosecuting federal crimes and for representing the government in civil cases, is the most frequent litigator in the federal court system. Several other executive branch agencies affect the operations of the courts. The United States Marshals Service, for example, provides security for federal courthouses and judges, and the General Services Administration builds and maintains federal courthouses.

Supreme Court of the United States

The United States Supreme Court consists of the Chief Justice of the United States and eight associate justices. At its discretion, and within certain guidelines established by Congress, the Supreme Court each year hears a limited number of the cases it is asked to decide. Those cases may begin in the federal or state courts, and they usually involve important questions about the Constitution or federal law.

Courts of Appeals

The 94 U.S. judicial districts are organized into 12 regional circuits, each of which has a United States court of appeals. A court of appeals hears appeals from the district courts located within its circuit, as well as appeals from decisions of federal administrative agencies.

In addition, the Court of Appeals for the Federal Circuit has nationwide jurisdiction to hear appeals in specialized cases, such as those involving patent laws and cases decided by the Court of International Trade and the Court of Federal Claims.

Bankruptcy Appellate Panels

Bankruptcy Appellate Panels (BAPs) are 3-judge panels authorized to hear appeals of bankruptcy court decisions. These panels are a unit of the federal courts of appeals.

BAPs were established under the Bankruptcy Reform Acts of 1978 and 1994. 28 U.S.C. §158 sets forth jurisdiction for appeals of bankruptcy decisions and authorizes the establishment of BAPs upon the order of the circuit judicial councils. BAP judges continue to serve as active bankruptcy judges in addition to their duties on the appellate panel.

Appeals from dispositive orders of bankruptcy judges may be taken to the district court or the BAP (if one has been established and the district has chosen to participate), with further appeal as of right to the court of appeals for the circuit. The BAP will hear an appeal of a bankruptcy court decision, unless one of the parties to the appeal makes a proper and timely election to have the appeal heard by the district court in accordance with requirements of federal statutes and procedural rules.

The following circuits have established BAPs:

1st, 6th, 8th, 9th, and 10th Circuits.

District Courts

The United States district courts are the trial courts of the federal court system. Within limits set by Congress and the Constitution, the district courts have jurisdiction to hear nearly all categories of federal cases, including both civil and criminal matters. Every day hundreds of people across the nation are selected for jury duty and help decide some of these cases.

There are 94 federal judicial districts, including at least one district in each state, the District of Columbia and Puerto Rico. Three territories of the United States -- the Virgin Islands, Guam, and the Northern Mariana Islands -- have district courts that hear federal cases, including bankruptcy cases.

Bankruptcy courts are separate units of the district courts. Federal courts have exclusive jurisdiction over bankruptcy cases. This means that a bankruptcy case cannot be filed in a state court.

There are two special trial courts that have nationwide jurisdiction over certain types of cases.

1. The Court of International Trade addresses cases involving international trade and customs issues.

2. The United States Court of Federal Claims has jurisdiction over most claims for money damages against the United States, disputes over federal contracts, unlawful "takings" of private property by the federal government, and a variety of other claims against the United States.

Federal court reporters record proceedings and produce transcripts. The Court Reporter Statute, 28 U.S.C. § 753 sets forth the proceedings to be recorded including: (1) all proceedings in criminal cases had in open court; (2) all proceedings in other cases had in open court unless the parties with the approval of the judge shall agree specifically to the contrary; and (3) such other proceedings as a judge of the court may direct or as may be required by rule or order of court as may be requested by any party to the proceeding.

By law, each session of court and every proceeding designated by rule or order of the court or by one of the judges shall be recorded verbatim by shorthand, stenotype, stenomask, or electronic sound recording equipment. The method of recording may be elected by the district judge.

Transcripts

One of the primary responsibilities of the court reporter is to provide a written transcript of court proceedings upon the request of a party or order of court. Written transcripts are prepared within the Judicial Conference's guidelines on page format, page rates, and delivery schedules. The transcripts of proceedings recorded by electronic sound recording equipment are produced by private transcription services designated by the court to transcribe federal court proceedings.

The court reporters and transcribers may charge and collect fees for transcripts requested by the parties, including the United States. The fee schedule should be posted prominently in the district court clerk's office or available on a court's web site. When a transcript is ordered, the first party to order it pays the original transcript rate, and subsequent requesters pay a copy rate (see Maximum Transcript Rates). When a court reporter or transcriber delivers the original transcript to the ordering party, the court reporter or transcriber is also required to file a certified electronic copy to the clerk of court.

The Judicial Conference has made it explicit that official court reporters may charge only copy fees for transcripts provided to parties when the original transcript was produced at the request of a judge.

The Judicial Conference approved a policy regarding the availability of transcripts of court proceedings filed with the clerk of court in electronic format. A transcript provided to a court by a court reporter or transcriber will be available at the office of the clerk of court for inspection only, for a period of 90 days (unless extended by the court) after it is delivered to the clerk. During the 90-day period:

- a copy of the transcript may be obtained from the court reporter or transcriber at the rate established by the Judicial Conference;

- the transcript will be available within the court for internal use; and

- an attorney who obtains the transcript from the court reporter or transcriber may obtain remote electronic access to the transcript through the court's Case Management/ Electronic Case Files (CM/ECF) system for purposes of creating hyperlinks to the transcript in court filings and for other purposes.

During the 90-day period (which may be extended by the court), access to the transcript in CM/ECF is restricted to court staff, public terminal users, attorneys of record or parties who have purchased the transcript from the court reporter/transcriber, and other persons as directed by the court (e.g., appellate attorneys). Also, during this time, parties may redact personal identifiers. After the 90-day period has ended, the filed transcript will be available for inspection and copying in the clerk's office and for download from the court's CM/ECF system through the judiciary's PACER system.

Contract Court Reporter Services

Under the Court Reporter Statute, the district courts may contract for court reporting services when necessary. Contract court reporters should be administered an oath for recording court proceedings.

Federal Court Interpreters

The use of competent federal court interpreters in proceedings involving speakers of languages other than English is critical to ensure that justice is carried out fairly for defendants and other stakeholders. The Court Interpreters Act, 28 U.S.C. §1827 provides that the Director of the Administrative Office of the United States Courts shall prescribe, determine, and certify the qualifications of persons who may serve as certified interpreters, when the Director considers certification of interpreters to be merited, for the hearing impaired (whether or not also speech impaired) and persons who speak only or primarily a language other than the English language, in judicial proceedings instituted by the United States.

The Administrative Office classifies three categories of interpreters:

- Certified interpreters

- Professionally qualified interpreter

- Language skilled interpreters

The professional knowledge, skills, and abilities required of a federal court interpreter are highly complex. Communication in courtroom proceedings may be more complex than that in other settings or in everyday life. For example, the parties involved may use specialized and legal terminology, formal and informal registers, dialect and jargon, varieties in language and nuances of meaning.

Three Categories of Interpreters

Certified interpreters

Certified interpreters have passed the Administrative Office certification examination. To date, certification programs have been developed for Spanish, Navajo and Haitian Creole. In these languages, the courts will select interpreters who have met the Administrative Office's criteria for certification if the judge determines that certified interpreters are reasonably available.

The Administrative Office's <u>Spanish-English Federal Court Interpreter Certification Examination</u> is administered in two phases. Candidates must pass the written exam in order to qualify to take an oral examination. The oral examination measures a candidate's ability to accurately perform simultaneous as well as consecutive interpretation and sight translations as encountered in the federal courts. The certification programs for Navajo and Haitian Creole are no longer offered.

For other languages, individuals may contact local federal courts to determine if that court has a need for the language of expertise. The <u>local federal court</u> will determine on a case-by-case basis whether the prospective interpreter is either professionally qualified or language skilled. In languages other than Spanish, Navajo and Haitian-Creole, interpreters are designated as:

- professionally qualified and
- language skilled.

Professionally qualified interpreters

The category of professionally qualified (P.Q.) interpreters applies to all languages, except those for which the AO has certified interpreters (Spanish, Navajo, and Haitian Creole). Credentials for professionally qualified interpreters require sufficient documentation and authentication, and must meet the criteria in one of the following:

(a) Passed the U.S. Department of State conference or seminar interpreter test in a language pair that includes English and the target language. The U.S. Department of State's escort interpreter test is not accepted as qualifying.

(b) Passed the interpreter test of the United Nations in a language pair that includes English and the target language.

(c) Is a current member in good standing of:

(1) the <u>Association Internationale des Interprètes de Conférence (AIIC)</u>; or

(2) The <u>American Association of Language Specialists (TAALS)</u>.

The language pair of the membership qualification must be English and the target language.

(d) For sign language interpreters, someone who holds the Specialist Certificate: Legal (SC:L) of the
<u>Registry of Interpreters for the Deaf (RID)</u>.

Language Skilled/*Ad Hoc* interpreters

An Interpreter who does not qualify as a professionally qualified interpreter, but who can demonstrate to the satisfaction of the court the ability to interpret court proceedings from English to a designated language and from that language into English, will be classified as a language skilled/*ad hoc* interpreter. Certified and professionally qualified interpreters are paid at a higher rate than language skilled/*ad hoc* interpreters.

Court Interpreter Knowledge, Skills, and Abilities

Interpreter skills include:

- Highly proficient in both English and the other language.

- Impartiality.

- Able to accurately and idiomatically turn the message from the source language into the receptor language without any additions, omissions or other misleading factors that alter the intended meaning of the message from the speaker.

- Adept at simultaneous interpretation, which is the most frequent form of interpretation used in the courtroom, and in consecutive interpretation and sight translation.

- Able to communicate orally including appropriate delivery and poise.

- Demonstrates high professional standards for courtroom demeanor and professional conduct.

The single greatest operational requirement in the federal courts is for Spanish-language interpreters. However, there is also a need for interpreters in other languages, including Chinese (Mandarin, Cantonese, and Foochow), Portuguese, Vietnamese, Korean, Russian, and Arabic.

The need for specific language interpreters is determined by the local district courts and not by the Administrative Office. However, in accordance with the Court Interpreters Act, the Administrative Office establishes the standards and guidelines for selecting and using interpreters in federal court proceedings.

Bankruptcy Courts

Each of the 94 federal judicial districts handles bankruptcy matters, and in almost all districts, bankruptcy cases are filed in the bankruptcy court. Bankruptcy cases cannot be filed in state court. Bankruptcy laws help people who can no longer pay their creditors get a fresh start by liquidating their assets to pay their debts, or by creating a repayment plan.

Bankruptcy laws also protect troubled businesses and provide for orderly distributions to business creditors through reorganization or liquidation. These procedures are covered under Title 11 of the United States Code (the Bankruptcy Code). The vast majority of cases are filed under the three main chapters of the Bankruptcy Code, which are Chapter 7, Chapter 11, and Chapter 13.

Civil Cases

A federal civil case involves a legal dispute between two or more parties. To begin a civil lawsuit in federal court, the plaintiff files a complaint with the court and "serves" a copy of the complaint on the defendant. The complaint describes the plaintiff's injury, explains how the defendant caused the injury, and asks the court to order relief. A plaintiff may seek money to compensate for the injury, or may ask the court to order the defendant to stop the conduct that is causing the harm. The court may also order other types of relief, such as a declaration of the legal rights of the plaintiff in a particular situation.

To avoid the expense of having a trial, judges encourage the litigants to try to reach an agreement resolving their dispute.

To prepare a case for trial, the litigants may conduct "discovery." In discovery, the litigants must provide information to each other about the case, such as the identity of witnesses and copies of any documents related to the case. The purpose of discovery is to prepare for trial by requiring the litigants to assemble their evidence and prepare to call witnesses. Each side also may file requests, or "motions," with the court seeking rulings on the discovery of evidence, or on the procedures to be followed at trial.

One common method of discovery is the deposition. In a deposition, a witness is required under oath to answer questions about the case asked by the lawyers in the presence of a court reporter. The court reporter is a person specially trained to record all testimony and produce a word-for-word account called a transcript.

To avoid the expense and delay of having a trial, judges encourage the litigants to try to reach an agreement resolving their dispute. In particular, the courts encourage the use of mediation, arbitration, and other forms of alternative dispute resolution, or "ADR," designed to produce an early resolution of a dispute without the need for trial or other court proceedings. As a result, litigants often decide to resolve a civil lawsuit with an agreement known as a "settlement."

If a case is not settled, the court will schedule a trial. In a wide variety of civil cases, either side is entitled under the Constitution to request a jury trial. If the parties waive their right to a jury, then the case will be heard by a judge without a jury.

At a trial, witnesses testify under the supervision of a judge. By applying rules of evidence, the judge determines which information may be presented in the courtroom. To ensure that witnesses speak from their own knowledge and do not change their story based on what they hear another witness say, witnesses are kept out of the courtroom until it is time for them to testify.

A court reporter keeps a record of the trial proceedings.

A deputy clerk of court also keeps a record of each person who testifies and marks for the record any documents, photographs, or other items introduced into evidence.

As the questioning of a witness proceeds, the opposing attorney may object to a question if it invites the witness to say something that is not based on the witness's personal knowledge, is unfairly prejudicial, or is irrelevant to the case. The judge rules on the objection, generally by ruling that it is either sustained or overruled. If the objection is sustained, the witness is not required to answer the question, and the attorney must move on to his next question. The court reporter records the objections so that a court of appeals can review the arguments later if necessary.

At the conclusion of the evidence, each side gives a closing argument. In a jury trial, the judge will explain the law that is relevant to the case and the decisions the jury needs to make. The jury generally is asked to determine whether the defendant is responsible for harming the plaintiff in some way, and then to determine the amount of damages that the defendant will be required to pay. If the case is being tried before a judge without a jury, known as a "bench" trial, the judge will decide these issues. In a civil case the plaintiff must convince the jury by a "preponderance of the evidence" (i.e., that it is more likely than not) that the defendant is responsible for the harm the plaintiff has suffered.

Criminal Cases

The judicial process in a criminal case differs from a civil case in several important ways. At the beginning of a federal criminal case, the principal actors are the U.S. attorney (the prosecutor) and the grand jury. The U.S. attorney represents the United States in most court proceedings, including all criminal prosecutions. The grand jury reviews evidence presented by the U.S. attorney and decides whether there is sufficient evidence to require a defendant to stand trial.

After a person is arrested, a pretrial services or probation officer of the court immediately interviews the defendant and conducts an investigation of the defendant's background. The information obtained by the pretrial services or probation office will be used to help a judge decide whether to release the defendant into the community before trial, and whether to impose conditions of release.

The standard of proof in a criminal trial is "beyond a reasonable doubt," which means the evidence must be so strong that there is no reasonable doubt that the defendant committed the crime.

At an initial appearance, a judge advises the defendant of the charges filed, considers whether the defendant should be held in jail until trial, and determines whether there is probable cause to believe that an offense has been committed and the defendant has committed it. Defendants who are unable to afford counsel are advised of their right to a court-appointed attorney. The court may appoint either a federal public defender or a private attorney who has agreed to accept such appointments from the court. In either type of appointment, the attorney will be paid by the court from funds appropriated by Congress. Defendants released into the community before trial may be required to obey certain restrictions, such as home confinement or drug testing, and to make periodic reports to a pretrial services officer to ensure appearance at trial.

The defendant enters a plea to the charges brought by the U.S. attorney at a hearing known as an arraignment. Most defendants — more than 90% — plead guilty rather than go to trial. If a defendant pleads guilty in return for the government agreeing to drop certain charges or to recommend a lenient sentence, the agreement often is called a "plea bargain." If the defendant pleads guilty, the judge may impose a sentence at that time, but more commonly will schedule a hearing to determine the sentence at a later date. In most felony cases the judge waits for the results of a presentence report, prepared by the court's probation office, before imposing sentence. If the defendant pleads not guilty, the judge will proceed to schedule a trial.

Criminal cases include a limited amount of pretrial discovery proceedings similar to those in civil cases, with substantial restrictions to protect the identity of government informants and to prevent intimidation of witnesses. The attorneys also may file motions, which are requests for rulings by the court before the trial. For example, defense attorneys often file a motion to suppress evidence, which asks the court to exclude from the trial evidence that the defendant believes was obtained by the government in violation of the defendant's constitutional rights.

In a criminal trial, the burden of proof is on the government. Defendants do not have to prove their innocence. Instead, the government must provide evidence to convince the jury of the defendant's guilt. The standard of proof in a criminal trial is proof "beyond a reasonable doubt," which means the evidence must be so strong that there is no reasonable doubt that the defendant committed the crime.

If a defendant is found not guilty, the defendant is released and the government may not appeal. Nor can the person be charged again with the same crime in a federal court. The Constitution prohibits "double jeopardy," or being tried twice for the same offense.

If the verdict is guilty, the judge determines the defendant's sentence according to special federal sentencing guidelines issued by the United States Sentencing Commission. The court's probation office prepares a report for the court that applies the sentencing guidelines to the individual defendant and the crimes for which he or she has been found guilty. During sentencing, the court may consider not only the evidence produced at trial, but all relevant information that may be provided by the pretrial services officer, the U.S. attorney, and the defense attorney. In unusual circumstances, the court may depart from the sentence calculated according to the sentencing guidelines.

A sentence may include time in prison, a fine to be paid to the government, and restitution to be paid to crime victims. The court's probation officers assist the court in enforcing any conditions that are imposed as part of a criminal sentence. The supervision of offenders also may involve services such as substance abuse testing and treatment programs, job counseling, and alternative detention options.

Civil Cases | Criminal Cases | Bankruptcy Cases | The Appeals Process

Bankruptcy Cases

Federal courts have exclusive jurisdiction over bankruptcy cases. This means that a bankruptcy case cannot be filed in a state court.

The primary purposes of the law of bankruptcy are

- to give an honest debtor a "fresh start" in life by relieving the debtor of most debts, and

- to repay creditors in an orderly manner to the extent that the debtor has property available for payment.

Some bankruptcy cases are filed to allow a debtor to reorganize and establish a plan to repay creditors, while other cases involve liquidation of the debtor's property.

A bankruptcy case normally begins by the debtor filing a petition with the bankruptcy court. A petition may be filed by an individual, by a husband and wife together, or by a corporation or other entity. The debtor is also required to file statements listing assets, income, liabilities, and the names and addresses of all creditors and how much they are owed. The filing of the petition automatically prevents, or "stays," debt collection actions against the debtor and the debtor's property. As long as the stay remains in effect, creditors cannot bring or continue lawsuits, make wage garnishments, or even make telephone calls demanding payment. Creditors receive notice from the clerk of court that the debtor has filed a bankruptcy petition. Some bankruptcy cases are filed to allow a debtor to reorganize and establish a plan to repay creditors, while other cases involve liquidation of the debtor's property. In many bankruptcy cases involving liquidation of the property of individual consumers, there is little or no money available from the debtor's estate to pay creditors. As a result, in these cases there are few issues or disputes, and the debtor is normally granted a "discharge" of most debts without objection. This means that the debtor will no longer be personally liable for repaying the debts.

In other cases, however, disputes may give rise to litigation in a bankruptcy case over such matters as who owns certain property, how it should be used, what the property is worth, how much is owed on a debt, whether the debtor should be discharged from certain debts, or how much money should be paid to lawyers, accountants, auctioneers, or other professionals. Litigation in the bankruptcy court is conducted in much the same way that civil cases are handled in the district court. There may be discovery, pretrial proceedings, settlement efforts, and a trial.

The Appeals Process

The losing party in a decision by a trial court in the federal system normally is entitled to appeal the decision to a federal court of appeals. Similarly, a litigant who is not satisfied with a decision made by a federal administrative agency usually may file a petition for review of the agency decision by a court of appeals. Judicial review in cases involving certain federal agencies or programs — for example, disputes over Social Security benefits — may be obtained first in a district court rather than a court of appeals.

In a civil case either side may appeal the verdict. In a criminal case, the defendant may appeal a guilty verdict, but the government may not appeal if a defendant is found not guilty. Either side in a criminal case may appeal with respect to the sentence that is imposed after a guilty verdict.

In a criminal case, the defendant may appeal a guilty verdict, but the government may not appeal if a defendant is found not guilty.

In most bankruptcy courts, an appeal of a ruling by a bankruptcy judge may be taken to the district court. Several courts of appeals, however, have established a bankruptcy appellate panel consisting of three bankruptcy judges to hear appeals directly from the bankruptcy courts. In either situation, the party that loses in the initial bankruptcy appeal may then appeal to the court of appeals.

A litigant who files an appeal, known as an "appellant," must show that the trial court or administrative agency made a legal error that affected the decision in the case. The court of appeals makes its decision based on the record of the case established by the trial court or agency. It does not receive additional evidence or hear witnesses. The court of appeals also may review the factual findings of the trial court or agency, but typically may only overturn a decision on factual grounds if the findings were "clearly erroneous."

The court of appeals decision usually will be the last word in a case, unless it sends the case back to the trial court for additional proceedings, or the parties ask the U.S. Supreme Court to review the case.

Appeals are decided by panels of three judges working together. The appellant presents legal arguments to the panel, in writing, in a document called a "brief." In the brief, the appellant tries to persuade the judges that the trial court made an error, and that its decision should be reversed. On the other hand, the party defending against the appeal, known as the "appellee," tries in its brief to show why the trial court decision was correct, or why any error made by the trial court was not significant enough to affect the outcome of the case.

Although some cases are decided on the basis of written briefs alone, many cases are selected for an "oral argument" before the court. Oral argument in the court of appeals is a structured discussion between the appellate lawyers and the panel of judges focusing on the legal principles in dispute. Each side is given a short time — usually about 15 minutes — to present arguments to the court.

The court of appeals decision usually will be the final word in the case, unless it sends the case back to the trial court for additional proceedings, or the parties ask the U.S. Supreme Court to review the case. In some cases the decision may be reviewed en banc, that is, by a larger group of judges (usually all) of the court of appeals for the circuit.

A litigant who loses in a federal court of appeals, or in the highest court of a state, may file a petition for a "writ of certiorari," which is a document asking the Supreme Court to review the case. The Supreme Court, however, does not have to grant review. The Court typically will agree to hear a case only when it involves an unusually important legal principle, or when two or more federal appellate courts have interpreted a law differently. There are also a small number of special circumstances in which the Supreme Court is required by law to hear an appeal. When the Supreme Court hears a case, the parties are required to file written briefs and the Court may hear oral argument.

Federal Courts & the Public

With certain very limited exceptions, each step of the federal judicial process is open to the public. Many federal courthouses are historic buildings, and all are designed to inspire in the public a respect for the tradition and purpose of the American judicial process.

An individual citizen who wishes to observe a court in session may go to the federal courthouse, check the court calendar, and watch a proceeding. Anyone may review the pleadings and other papers in a case by going to the clerk of court's office and asking for the appropriate case file. Unlike most of the state courts, however, the federal courts generally do not permit television or radio coverage of trial court proceedings.

Court dockets and some case files are available on the Internet through the Public Access to Court Electronic Records system (known as PACER), at www.pacer.gov. In addition, nearly every federal court maintains a web site with information about court rules and procedures.

The right of public access to court proceedings is partly derived from the Constitution and partly from court tradition. By conducting their judicial work in public view, judges enhance public confidence in the courts, and they allow citizens to learn first-hand how our judicial system works.

In a few situations the public may not have full access to court records and court proceedings. In a high-profile trial, for example, there may not be enough space in the courtroom to accommodate everyone who would like to observe. Access to the courtroom also may be restricted for security or privacy reasons, such as the protection of a juvenile or a confidential informant. Finally, certain documents may be placed under seal by the judge, meaning that they are not available to the public. Examples of sealed information include confidential business records, certain law enforcement reports, and juvenile records.

The Supreme Court of the United States

The Supreme Court is the highest court in the federal Judiciary. Congress has established two levels of federal courts under the Supreme Court: the trial courts and the appellate courts.

The United States Supreme Court consists of the Chief Justice of the United States and eight associate justices. At its discretion, and within certain guidelines established by Congress, the Supreme Court each year hears a limited number of the cases it is asked to decide. Those cases may begin in the federal or state courts, and they usually involve important questions about the Constitution or federal law.

District (Trial) Courts

The United States district courts are the trial courts of the federal court system. Within limits set by Congress and the Constitution, the district courts have jurisdiction to hear nearly all categories of federal cases, including both civil and criminal matters. There are 94 federal judicial districts, including at least one district in each state, the District of Columbia and Puerto Rico. Each district includes a United States bankruptcy court as a unit of the district court. Three territories of the United States — the Virgin Islands, Guam, and the Northern Mariana Islands — have district courts that hear federal cases, including bankruptcy cases.

There are two special trial courts that have nationwide jurisdiction over certain types of cases. The Court of International Trade addresses cases involving international trade and customs issues. The United States Court of Federal Claims has jurisdiction over most claims for monetary damages against the United States, disputes over federal contracts, unlawful "taking" of private property by the federal government, and a variety of other claims against the United States.

Appellate Courts

The 94 judicial districts are organized into 12 regional circuits, each of which has a United States court of appeals. A court of appeals hears appeals from the district courts located within its circuit, as well as appeals from decisions of federal administrative agencies. In addition, the Court of Appeals for the Federal Circuit has nationwide jurisdiction to hear appeals in specialized cases, such as those involving patent laws and cases decided by the Court of International Trade and the Court of Federal Claims.

Although federal courts are located in every state, they are not the only forum available to potential litigants. In fact, the great majority of legal disputes in American courts are addressed in the separate state court systems.

For example, state courts handle cases involving

- divorce and child custody matter;

- probate and inheritance issues;

- real estate questions, and juvenile matters; and

- most criminal cases, contract disputes, traffic violations, and personal injury cases.

Federal courts hear cases involving

- the constitutionality of a law;

- cases involving the laws and treaties of the U.S.;

- ambassadors and public ministers;

- disputes between two or more states;

- admiralty law; and

- bankruptcy cases.

In addition, certain categories of legal disputes may be resolved in special courts or entities that are part of the federal executive or legislative branches, and by state and federal administrative agencies.

Before a federal court can hear a case, or "exercise its jurisdiction," certain conditions must be met. First, under the Constitution, federal courts exercise only "judicial" powers. This means that federal judges may interpret the law only through the resolution of actual legal disputes, referred to in Article III of the Constitution as "Cases or Controversies." A court cannot attempt to correct a problem on its own initiative, or to answer a hypothetical legal question.

Second, assuming there is an actual case or controversy, the plaintiff in a federal lawsuit also must have legal "standing" to ask the court for a decision. That means the plaintiff must have been aggrieved, or legally harmed in some way, by the defendant.

Third, the case must present a category of dispute that the law in question was designed to address, and it must be a complaint that the court has the power to remedy. In other words, the court must be authorized, under the Constitution or a federal law, to hear the case and grant appropriate relief to the plaintiff. Finally, the case cannot be "moot," that is, it must present an ongoing problem for the court to resolve. The federal courts, thus, are courts of "limited" jurisdiction because they may only decide certain types of cases as provided by Congress or as identified in the Constitution.

Although the details of the complex web of federal jurisdiction that Congress has given the federal courts are beyond the scope of this brief guide, it is important to understand that there are two main sources of cases coming before the federal courts: "federal question" jurisdiction, and "diversity" jurisdiction.

In general, federal courts may decide cases that involve the United States government, the United States Constitution or federal laws, or controversies between states or between the United States and foreign governments. A case that raises such a "federal question" may be filed in federal court. Examples of such cases might include a claim by an individual for entitlement to money under a federal government program such as Social Security, a claim by the government that someone has violated federal laws, or a challenge to actions taken by a federal agency.

A case also may be filed in federal court based on the "diversity of citizenship" of the litigants, such as between citizens of different states, or between United States citizens and those of another country. To ensure fairness to the out-of-state litigant, the Constitution provides that such cases may be heard in a federal court. An important limit to diversity jurisdiction is that only cases involving more than $75,000 in potential damages may be filed in a federal court. Claims below that amount may only be pursued in state court. Moreover, any diversity jurisdiction case, regardless of the amount of money involved, may be brought in a state court rather than a federal court.

Federal courts also have jurisdiction over all bankruptcy matters, which Congress has determined should be addressed in federal courts rather than the state courts. Through the bankruptcy process, individuals or businesses that can no longer pay their creditors may either seek a court-supervised liquidation of their assets, or they may reorganize their financial affairs and work out a plan to pay off their debts.

Although federal courts are located in every state, they are not the only forum available to potential litigants. In fact, the great majority of legal disputes in American courts are addressed in the separate state court systems. For example, state courts have jurisdiction over virtually all divorce and child custody matters, probate and inheritance issues, real estate questions, and juvenile matters, and they handle most criminal cases, contract disputes, traffic violations, and personal injury cases. In addition, certain categories of legal disputes may be resolved in special courts or entities that are part of the federal executive or legislative branches, and by state and federal administrative agencies.

Comparing State & Federal Courts

Discover the differences in structure, judicial selection, and cases heard in each system.

The U.S. Constitution is the supreme law of the land in the United States. It creates a federal system of government in which power is shared between the federal government and the state governments. Due to federalism, both the federal government and each of the state governments have their own court systems.

The Federal Court System

The State Court System

STRUCTURE

- Article III of the Constitution invests the judicial power of the United States in the federal court system. Article III, Section 1 specifically creates the U.S. Supreme Court and gives Congress the authority to create the lower federal courts.

- The Constitution and laws of each state establish the state courts. A court of last resort, often known as a Supreme Court, is usually the highest court. Some states also have an intermediate Court of Appeals. Below these appeals courts are the state trial courts. Some are referred to as Circuit or District Courts.

- Congress has used this power to establish the 13 U.S. Courts of Appeals, the 94 U.S. District Courts, the U.S. Court of Claims, and the U.S. Court of International Trade. U.S. Bankruptcy Courts handle bankruptcy cases. Magistrate

- States also usually have courts that handle specific legal matters, e.g., probate court (wills and estates); juvenile court; family court; etc.

Judges handle some District
Court matters.

- Parties dissatisfied with a
  decision of a U.S. District
  Court, the U.S. Court of Claims,
  and/or the U.S. Court of
  International Trade may
  appeal to a U.S. Court of
  Appeals.

- Parties dissatisfied with the
  decision of the trial court may
  take their case to the
  intermediate Court of Appeals.

- A party may ask the U.S.
  Supreme Court to review a
  decision of the U.S. Court of
  Appeals, but the Supreme
  Court usually is under no
  obligation to do so. The U.S.
  Supreme Court is the final
  arbiter of federal
  constitutional questions.

- Parties have the option to ask
  the highest state court to hear
  the case.

- Only certain cases are eligible
  for review by the U.S. Supreme
  Court.

SELECTION OF JUDGES

The Constitution states that federal judges are to be nominated by the President and confirmed by the Senate.

They hold office during good behavior, typically, for life. Through Congressional impeachment proceedings, federal judges may be removed from office for misbehavior.

State court judges are selected in a variety of ways, including

- election,
- appointment for a given number of years,
- appointment for life, and
- combinations of these methods, e.g., appointment followed by election.

TYPES OF CASES HEARD

- Cases that deal with the constitutionality of a law
- Cases involving the laws and treaties of the U.S.
- Ambassadors and public ministers
- Disputes between two or more states
- Admiralty law, and
- Bankruptcy.

- Most criminal cases, probate (involving wills and estates)
- Most contract cases, tort cases (personal injuries), family law (marriages, divorces, adoptions), etc.

State courts are the final arbiters of state laws and constitutions. Their interpretation of federal law or the U.S. Constitution may be appealed to the U.S. Supreme Court. The Supreme Court may choose to hear or not to hear such cases.

ARTICLE I COURTS

Congress has created several Article I or legislative courts that do not have full judicial power. Judicial power is the authority to be the final decider in all questions of Constitutional law and all questions of federal law, and to hear claims at the core of habeas corpus issues.

- Article I courts are U.S. Court of Veterans' Appeals, the U.S. Court of Military Appeals, and the U.S. Tax Court.

Cases in Federal and State Courts

Find out what types of cases are heard in federal courts and state courts. How are they different? How are they similar?

State Courts

Crimes under state legislation.

State constitutional issues and cases involving state laws or regulations.

Family law issues.

Real property issues.

Most private contract disputes (except those resolved under bankruptcy law).

Most issues involving the regulation of trades and professions.

Most professional malpractice issues.

Most issues involving the internal governance of

Federal Courts

Crimes under statuses enacted by Congress.

Most cases involving federal laws or regulations (for example: tax, Social Security, broadcasting, civil rights).

Matters involving interstate and international commerce, including airline and railroad regulation.

Cases involving securities and commodities regulation, including takeover of publicly held corporations.

Admiralty cases.

State or Federal Courts

Crimes punishable under both federal and state law.

Federal constitutional issues.

Certain civil rights claims.

"Class action" cases.

Environmental regulations.

Certain disputes involving federal law.

business associations such as partnerships and corporations.

Most personal injury lawsuits.

Most workers' injury claims.

Probate and inheritance matters.

Most traffic violations and registration of motor vehicles.

International trade law matters.

Patent, copyright, and other intellectual property issues.

Cases involving rights under treaties, foreign states, and foreign nationals.

State law disputes when "diversity of citizenship" exists.

Bankruptcy matters.

Disputes between states.

Habeas corpus actions.

Traffic violations and other misdemeanors occurring on certain federal property.

The United States Federal Courts

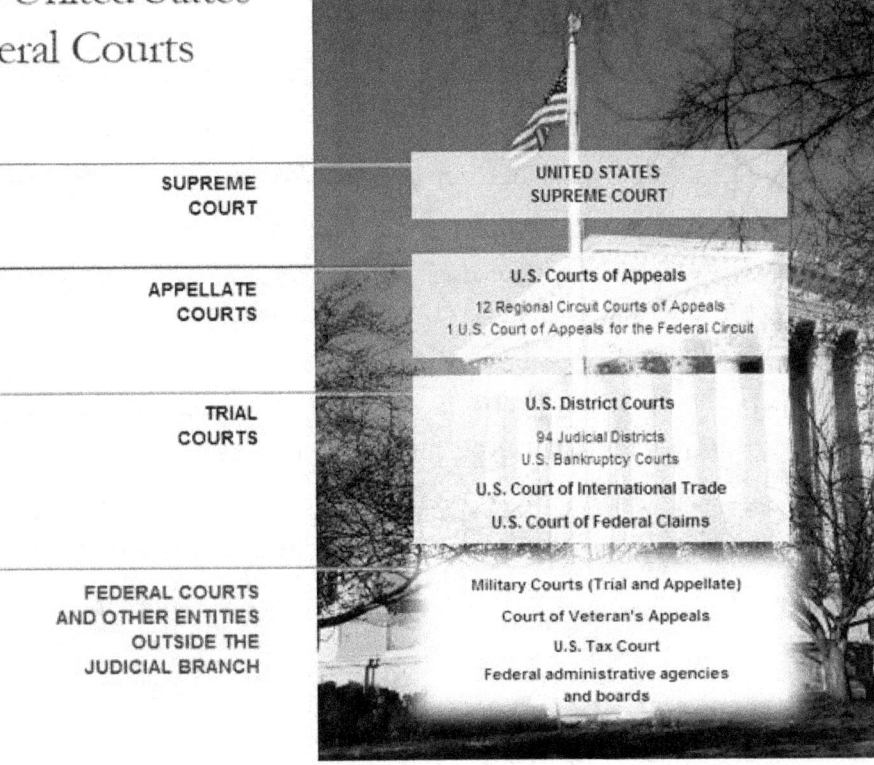

SUPREME COURT — UNITED STATES SUPREME COURT

APPELLATE COURTS — U.S. Courts of Appeals
12 Regional Circuit Courts of Appeals
1 U.S. Court of Appeals for the Federal Circuit

TRIAL COURTS — U.S. District Courts
94 Judicial Districts
U.S. Bankruptcy Courts

U.S. Court of International Trade

U.S. Court of Federal Claims

FEDERAL COURTS AND OTHER ENTITIES OUTSIDE THE JUDICIAL BRANCH — Military Courts (Trial and Appellate)
Court of Veteran's Appeals
U.S. Tax Court
Federal administrative agencies and boards

Jury Service in Federal Court

Importance, History, and Constitutional Foundations of Jury Service

- Jury service is a direct means for citizens to participate in the judicial process. Jurors make decisions that have an impact on individuals' lives, property, and liberty.

- The jury, as an institution, has a long and distinguished history. As early as the English Magna Carta (1215), it was hailed as the protector of individual rights and liberties.

- In the U.S. Constitution the <u>Sixth Amendment</u> (OurDocuments.gov) provides for impartial jury trials in criminal cases.

- The <u>Fifth Amendment</u> (OurDocuments.gov) guarantees the right to a grand jury indictment.

- The <u>Seventh Amendment</u> (OurDocuments.gov) provides for juries in certain civil cases.

Legal, Financial, and Personal Concerns of Prospective Jurors

- Society considers jury duty so important to running a democracy that the failure to report to the courthouse when summoned can result in a fine and/or imprisonment.

- The law relating to federal jury service is 28 U.S.C. SS §§1861 et. seq.

- Federal law prohibits employers from firing or taking adverse action against individuals for participating in jury service.

- Federal law also provides a daily stipend for federal jurors and makes provisions for reimbursements for certain travel expenses.

- Sign language interpreters are available to deaf and hearing-impaired potential jurors. Other auxiliary aides also are available.

- In order to enhance jurors' comprehension of the issues during the trial, some courts permit jurors to take notes or submit written questions they would like the lawyers to ask witnesses.

- Jurors must not discuss the case with anyone except fellow jurors throughout the trial process. After the trial, jurors are under no obligation to talk about their experience with others, including the media. Jurors also are not prohibited from talking about their jury experience. Each juror has a choice.

Reporting to the Right Courthouse: Federal and State Courts

- There are two different court systems within the United States, the federal court system and the state court systems. In the federal system, there are 94 district (trial) courts, and 12 Circuit Courts of Appeals in regions across the country. In each state, there is one state court system that has courthouses in towns and cities throughout the state.

- The federal court system hears cases based on the U.S. Constitution and statutes passed by Congress. The state court system hears cases based on state constitutions and statutes passed by state legislatures. The federal courts do not hear cases involving only state law.

What Kind of Jury: Grand Jury or Petit Jury?

- There are two types of jury systems in the United States, the grand jury and the petit jury.

- The grand jury consists of 23 citizens of which 16 must be present to constitute a quorum for the transaction of business. Grand jurors analyze the evidence presented by a government attorney and then decide, based on this evidence, whether to indict (charge) an individual with a crime. Twelve or more grand jurors must vote in favor of the indictment before it may be returned.

- A petit jury is a body of six to 12 citizens, and alternate jurors, that hears a criminal or civil case and decides the facts of the case. Unless otherwise noted, the term jury refers to a petit jury.

From the Jury Pool to the Jury Box: Voir Dire

- Not every person summoned to jury duty is selected to participate on a jury. During a process called *voir dire*, the trial judge and/or the lawyers for each side question potential jurors for bias.

- Each side has a certain number of peremptory challenges and an unlimited number of challenges for cause. A peremptory challenge allows a lawyer to dismiss a potential juror for any reason. A challenge for cause allows a party to dismiss a potential juror for possible biases.

The Job of the Judge, the Job of the Jury

- The judge and the jury have specific roles in a judicial proceeding. The judge determines the appropriate law that should be applied to the case and the jury finds the facts in the case.

- At the end of the trial, the judge instructs the jury on the applicable law. While the jury must obey the judge's instructions as to the law, the jury alone is responsible for determining the facts of the case.

What Kind of Case: Criminal or Civil - What's the Difference?

- There are two types of judicial proceedings in the federal courts, criminal and civil cases.

- In a criminal trial, an individual is accused of committing an offense - a crime - against society as a whole. Criminal juries consist of 12 jurors and alternates and a unanimous decision must be reached before a defendant is found "guilty." The burden of proof is on the government and the standard is "beyond a reasonable doubt."

- In a civil trial, litigants are seeking remedies for private wrongs that don't, necessarily, have a broader social impact. Civil juries must consist of at least six jurors and the verdict must be unanimous unless the parties stipulate otherwise. The standard of proof is a "preponderance of the evidence," or "more true than not." Not all civil cases are heard by jurors; some are conducted before a judge.

- Guilty pleas and plea negotiations reduce the need for juries in criminal cases, and settlement negotiations reduce the need for juries in civil cases. Negotiations and settlements are effective avenues the courts and the parties use to arrive at justice.

A

Acquittal

A jury verdict that a criminal defendant is not guilty, or the finding of a judge that the evidence is insufficient to support a conviction.

Active judge

A judge in the full-time service of the court. Compare to senior judge.

Administrative Office of the United States Courts (AO)

The federal agency responsible for collecting court statistics, administering the federal courts' budget, and performing many other administrative and programmatic functions, under the direction and supervision of the Judicial Conference of the United States.

Admissible

A term used to describe evidence that may be considered by a jury or judge in civil and criminal cases.

Adversary proceeding

A lawsuit arising in or related to a bankruptcy case that begins by filing a complaint with the court, that is, a "trial" that takes place within the context of a bankruptcy case.

Affidavit

A written or printed statement made under oath.

Affirmed

In the practice of the court of appeals, it means that the court of appeals has concluded that the lower court decision is correct and will stand as rendered by the lower court.

Alternate juror

A juror selected in the same manner as a regular juror who hears all the evidence but does not help decide the case unless called on to replace a regular juror.

Alternative dispute resolution (ADR)

A procedure for settling a dispute outside the courtroom. Most forms of ADR are not binding, and involve referral of the case to a neutral party such as an arbitrator or mediator.

Amicus curiae

Latin for "friend of the court." It is advice formally offered to the court in a brief filed by an entity interested in, but not a party to, the case.

Answer

The formal written statement by a defendant in a civil case that responds to a complaint, articulating the grounds for defense.

Appeal

A request made after a trial by a party that has lost on one or more issues that a higher court review the decision to determine if it was correct. To make such a request is "to appeal" or "to take an appeal." One who appeals is called the "appellant;" the other party is the "appellee."

Appellant

The party who appeals a district court's decision, usually seeking reversal of that decision.

Appellate

About appeals; an appellate court has the power to review the judgment of a lower court (trial court) or tribunal. For example, the U.S. circuit courts of appeals review the decisions of the U.S. district courts.

Appellee

The party who opposes an appellant's appeal, and who seeks to persuade the appeals court to affirm the district court's decision.

Arraignment

A proceeding in which a criminal defendant is brought into court, told of the charges in an indictment or information, and asked to plead guilty or not guilty.

Article III judge

A federal judge who is appointed for life, during "good behavior," under Article III of the Constitution. Article III judges are nominated by the President and confirmed by the Senate.

Assets

Property of all kinds, including real and personal, tangible and intangible.

Assume

An agreement to continue performing duties under a contract or lease.

Automatic stay

An injunction that automatically stops lawsuits, foreclosures, garnishments, and most collection activities against the debtor the moment a bankruptcy petition is filed.

B

Bail

The release, prior to trial, of a person accused of a crime, under specified conditions designed to assure that person's appearance in court when required. Also can refer to the amount of bond money posted as a financial condition of pretrial release.

Bankruptcy

A legal procedure for dealing with debt problems of individuals and businesses; specifically, a case filed under one of the chapters of title 11 of the United States Code (the Bankruptcy Code).

Bankruptcy administrator

An officer of the Judiciary serving in the judicial districts of Alabama and North Carolina who, like the United States trustee, is responsible for supervising the administration of bankruptcy cases, estates, and trustees; monitoring plans and disclosure statements; monitoring creditors' committees; monitoring fee applications; and performing other statutory duties.

Bankruptcy code

The informal name for title 11 of the United States Code (11 U.S.C. §§ 101-1330), the federal bankruptcy law.

Bankruptcy court

The bankruptcy judges in regular active service in each district; a unit of the district court.

Bankruptcy estate

All interests of the debtor in property at the time of the bankruptcy filing. The estate technically becomes the temporary legal owner of all of the debtor's property.

Bankruptcy judge

A judicial officer of the United States district court who is the court official with decision-making power over federal bankruptcy cases.

Bankruptcy petition

A formal request for the protection of the federal bankruptcy laws. (There is an official form for bankruptcy petitions.)

Bankruptcy trustee

A private individual or corporation appointed in all Chapter 7 and Chapter 13 cases to represent the interests of the bankruptcy estate and the debtor's creditors.

Bench trial

A trial without a jury, in which the judge serves as the fact-finder.

Brief

A written statement submitted in a trial or appellate proceeding that explains one side's legal and factual arguments.

Burden of proof

The duty to prove disputed facts. In civil cases, a plaintiff generally has the burden of proving his or her case. In criminal cases, the government has the burden of proving the defendant's guilt. (See standard of proof.)

Business bankruptcy

A bankruptcy case in which the debtor is a business or an individual involved in business and the debts are for business purposes.

C

Capital offense

A crime punishable by death.

Case file

A complete collection of every document filed in court in a case.

Case law

The law as established in previous court decisions. A synonym for legal precedent. Akin to common law, which springs from tradition and judicial decisions.

Caseload

The number of cases handled by a judge or a court.

Cause of action

A legal claim.

Chambers

The offices of a judge and his or her staff.

Chapter 7

The chapter of the Bankruptcy Code providing for "liquidation," that is, the sale of a debtor's nonexempt property and the distribution of the proceeds to creditors. In order to be eligible for Chapter 7, the debtor must satisfy a "means test." The court will evaluate the debtor's income and expenses to determine if the debtor may proceed under Chapter 7.

Chapter 7 trustee

A person appointed in a Chapter 7 case to represent the interests of the bankruptcy estate and the creditors. The trustee's responsibilities include reviewing the debtor's petition and schedules, liquidating the property of the estate, and making distributions to creditors. The trustee may also bring actions against creditors or the debtor to recover property of the bankruptcy estate.

Chapter 9

The chapter of the Bankruptcy Code providing for reorganization of municipalities (which includes cities and towns, as well as villages, counties, taxing districts, municipal utilities, and school districts).

Chapter 11

A reorganization bankruptcy, usually involving a corporation or partnership. A Chapter 11 debtor usually proposes a plan of reorganization to keep its business alive and pay creditors over time. Individuals or people in business can also seek relief in Chapter 11.

Chapter 12

The chapter of the Bankruptcy Code providing for adjustment of debts of a "family farmer" or "family fisherman," as the terms are defined in the Bankruptcy Code.

Chapter 13

The chapter of the Bankruptcy Code providing for the adjustment of debts of an individual with regular income, often referred to as a "wage-earner" plan. Chapter 13 allows a debtor to keep property and use his or her disposable income to pay debts over time, usually three to five years.

Chapter 13 trustee

A person appointed to administer a Chapter 13 case. A Chapter 13 trustee's responsibilities are similar to those of a Chapter 7 trustee; however, a Chapter 13 trustee has the additional responsibilities of overseeing the debtor's plan, receiving payments from debtors, and disbursing plan payments to creditors.

Chapter 15

The chapter of the Bankruptcy Code dealing with cases of cross-border insolvency.

Chief judge

The judge who has primary responsibility for the administration of a court; chief judges are determined by seniority.

Claim

A creditor's assertion of a right to payment from a debtor or the debtor's property.

Class action

A lawsuit in which one or more members of a large group, or class, of individuals or other entities sue on behalf of the entire class. The district court must find that the claims of the class members contain questions of law or fact in common before the lawsuit can proceed as a class action.

Clerk of court

The court officer who oversees administrative functions, especially managing the flow of cases through the court. The clerk's office is often called a court's central nervous system.

Collateral

Property that is promised as security for the satisfaction of a debt.

Common law

The legal system that originated in England and is now in use in the United States, which relies on the articulation of legal principles in a historical succession of judicial decisions. Common law principles can be changed by legislation.

Community service

A special condition the court imposes that requires an individual to work – without pay – for a civic or nonprofit organization.

Complaint

A written statement that begins a civil lawsuit, in which the plaintiff details the claims against the defendant.

Concurrent sentence

Prison terms for two or more offenses to be served at the same time, rather than one after the other. Example: Two five-year sentences and one three-year sentence, if served concurrently, result in a maximum of five years behind bars.

Confirmation

Approval of a plan of reorganization by a bankruptcy judge.

Consecutive sentence

Prison terms for two or more offenses to be served one after the other. Example: Two five-year sentences and one three-year sentence, if served consecutively, result in a maximum of 13 years behind bars.

Consumer bankruptcy

A bankruptcy case filed to reduce or eliminate debts that are primarily consumer debts.

Consumer debts

Debts incurred for personal, as opposed to business, needs.

Contingent claim

A claim that may be owed by the debtor under certain circumstances, e.g., where the debtor is a cosigner on another person's loan and that person fails to pay.

Contract

An agreement between two or more people that creates an obligation to do or not to do a particular thing.

Conviction

A judgment of guilt against a criminal defendant.

Counsel

Legal advice; a term also used to refer to the lawyers in a case.

Court

Government entity authorized to resolve legal disputes. Judges sometimes use "court" to refer to themselves in the third person, as in "the court has read the briefs."

Court reporter

A person who makes a word-for-word record of what is said in court, generally by using a stenographic machine, shorthand or audio recording, and then produces a transcript of the proceedings upon request.

Count

An allegation in an indictment or information, charging a defendant with a crime. An indictment or information may contain allegations that the defendant committed more than one crime. Each allegation is referred to as a count.

Creditor

A person to whom or business to which the debtor owes money or that claims to be owed money by the debtor.

Credit counseling

Generally refers to two events in individual bankruptcy cases: (1) the "individual or group briefing" from a nonprofit budget and credit counseling agency that individual debtors must attend prior to filing under any chapter of the Bankruptcy Code; and (2) the "instructional course in personal financial management" in chapters 7 and 13 that an individual debtor must complete before a discharge is entered. There are exceptions to both requirements for certain categories of debtors, exigent circumstances, or if the U.S. trustee or bankruptcy administrator have determined that there are insufficient approved credit counseling agencies available to provide the necessary counseling.

D

Damages

Money that a defendant pays a plaintiff in a civil case if the plaintiff has won. Damages may be compensatory (for loss or injury) or punitive (to punish and deter future misconduct).

Debtor

A person who has filed a petition for relief under the Bankruptcy Code.

Defendant

An individual (or business) against whom a lawsuit is filed.

Debtor's plan

A debtor's detailed description of how the debtor proposes to pay creditors' claims over a fixed period of time.

Declaratory judgment

A judge's statement about someone's rights. For example, a plaintiff may seek a declaratory judgment that a particular statute, as written, violates some constitutional right.

De facto

Latin, meaning "in fact" or "actually." Something that exists in fact but not as a matter of law.

Default judgment

A judgment awarding a plaintiff the relief sought in the complaint because the defendant has failed to appear in court or otherwise respond to the complaint.

Defendant

In a civil case, the person or organization against whom the plaintiff brings suit; in a criminal case, the person accused of the crime.

De jure

Latin, meaning "in law." Something that exists by operation of law.

De novo

Latin, meaning "anew." A trial de novo is a completely new trial. Appellate review de novo implies no deference to the trial judge's ruling.

Deposition

An oral statement made before an officer authorized by law to administer oaths. Such statements are often taken to examine potential witnesses, to obtain discovery, or to be used later in trial. See discovery.

Discharge

A release of a debtor from personal liability for certain dischargeable debts. Notable exceptions to dischargeability are taxes and student loans. A discharge releases a debtor from personal liability for certain debts known as dischargeable debts and prevents the creditors owed those debts from taking any action against the debtor or the debtor's property to collect the debts. The discharge also prohibits creditors from communicating with the debtor regarding the debt, including through telephone calls, letters, and personal contact.

Dischargeable debt

A debt for which the Bankruptcy Code allows the debtor's personal liability to be eliminated.

Disclosure statement

A written document prepared by the chapter 11 debtor or other plan proponent that is designed to provide "adequate information" to creditors to enable them to evaluate the chapter 11 plan of reorganization.

Discovery

Procedures used to obtain disclosure of evidence before trial.

Dismissal with prejudice

Court action that prevents an identical lawsuit from being filed later.

Dismissal without prejudice

Court action that allows the later filing.

Disposable income

Income not reasonably necessary for the maintenance or support of the debtor or dependents. If the debtor operates a business, disposable income is defined as those amounts over and above what is necessary for the payment of ordinary operating expenses.

Docket

A log containing the complete history of each case in the form of brief chronological entries summarizing the court proceedings.

Due process

In criminal law, the constitutional guarantee that a defendant will receive a fair and impartial trial. In civil law, the legal rights of someone who confronts an adverse action threatening liberty or property.

E

En banc

French, meaning "on the bench." All judges of an appellate court sitting together to hear a case, as opposed to the routine disposition by panels of three judges. In the Ninth Circuit, an en banc panel consists of 11 randomly selected judges.

Equitable

Pertaining to civil suits in "equity" rather than in "law." In English legal history, the courts of "law" could order the payment of damages and could afford no other remedy (see damages). A separate court of "equity" could order someone to do something or to cease to do something (e.g., injunction). In American jurisprudence, the federal courts have both legal and equitable power, but the distinction is still an important one. For example, a trial by jury is normally available in "law" cases but not in "equity" cases.

Equity

The value of a debtor's interest in property that remains after liens and other creditors' interests are considered. (Example: If a house valued at $60,000 is subject to a $30,000 mortgage, there is $30,000 of equity.)

Evidence

Information presented in testimony or in documents that is used to persuade the fact finder (judge or jury) to decide the case in favor of one side or the other.

Exclusionary rule

Doctrine that says evidence obtained in violation of a criminal defendant's constitutional or statutory rights is not admissible at trial.

Exculpatory evidence

Evidence indicating that a defendant did not commit the crime.

Executory contracts

Contracts or leases under which both parties to the agreement have duties remaining to be performed. If a contract or lease is executory, a debtor may assume it (keep the contract) or reject it (terminate the contract).

Exempt assets

Property that a debtor is allowed to retain, free from the claims of creditors who do not have liens on the property.

Exemptions, exempt property

Certain property owned by an individual debtor that the Bankruptcy Code or applicable state law permits the debtor to keep from unsecured creditors. For example, in some states the debtor may be able to exempt all or a portion of the equity in the debtor's primary residence (homestead exemption), or some or all "tools of the trade" used by the debtor to make a living (i.e., auto tools for an auto mechanic or dental tools for a dentist). The availability and amount of property the debtor may exempt depends on the state the debtor lives in.

Ex parte

A proceeding brought before a court by one party only, without notice to or challenge by the other side.

F

Face sheet filing

A bankruptcy case filed either without schedules or with incomplete schedules listing few creditors and debts. (Face sheet filings are often made for the purpose of delaying an eviction or foreclosure.)

Family farmer

An individual, individual and spouse, corporation, or partnership engaged in a farming operation that meets certain debt limits and other statutory criteria for filing a petition under Chapter 12.

Federal public defender

An attorney employed by the federal courts on a full-time basis to provide legal defense to defendants who are unable to afford counsel. The judiciary administers the federal defender program pursuant to the Criminal Justice Act.

Federal public defender organization

As provided for in the Criminal Justice Act, an organization established within a federal judicial circuit to represent criminal defendants who cannot afford an adequate defense. Each organization is supervised by a federal public defender appointed by the court of appeals for the circuit.

Federal question jurisdiction

Jurisdiction given to federal courts in cases involving the interpretation and application of the U.S. Constitution, acts of Congress, and treaties.

Felony

A serious crime, usually punishable by at least one year in prison.

File

To place a paper in the official custody of the clerk of court to enter into the files or records of a case.

Fraudulent transfer

A transfer of a debtor's property made with intent to defraud or for which the debtor receives less than the transferred property's value.

Fresh start

The characterization of a debtor's status after bankruptcy, i.e., free of most debts. (Giving debtors a fresh start is one purpose of the Bankruptcy Code.)

G

Grand jury

A body of 16-23 citizens who listen to evidence of criminal allegations, which is presented by the prosecutors, and determine whether there is probable cause to believe an individual committed an offense. See also indictment and U.S. attorney.

H

Habeas corpus

Latin, meaning "you have the body." A writ of habeas corpus generally is a judicial order forcing law enforcement authorities to produce a prisoner they are holding, and to justify the prisoner's continued confinement. Federal judges receive petitions for a writ of habeas corpus from state prison inmates who say their state prosecutions violated federally protected rights in some way.

Hearsay

Evidence presented by a witness who did not see or hear the incident in question but heard about it from someone else. With some exceptions, hearsay generally is not admissible as evidence at trial.

Home confinement

A special condition the court imposes that requires an individual to remain at home except for certain approved activities such as work and medical appointments. Home confinement may include the use of electronic monitoring equipment – a transmitter attached to the wrist or the ankle – to help ensure that the person stays at home as required.

I

Impeachment

1. The process of calling a witness's testimony into doubt. For example, if the attorney can show that the witness may have fabricated portions of his testimony, the witness is said to be "impeached;" 2. The constitutional process whereby the House of Representatives may "impeach" (accuse of misconduct) high officers of the federal government, who are then tried by the Senate.

In camera

Latin, meaning in a judge's chambers. Often means outside the presence of a jury and the public. In private.

Inculpatory evidence

Evidence indicating that a defendant did commit the crime.

Indictment

The formal charge issued by a grand jury stating that there is enough evidence that the defendant committed the crime to justify having a trial; it is used primarily for felonies. See also information.

In forma pauperis

"In the manner of a pauper." Permission given by the court to a person to file a case without payment of the required court fees because the person cannot pay them.

Information

A formal accusation by a government attorney that the defendant committed a misdemeanor. See also indictment.

Injunction

A court order preventing one or more named parties from taking some action. A preliminary injunction often is issued to allow fact-finding, so a judge can determine whether a permanent injunction is justified.

Insider (of corporate debtor)

A director, officer, or person in control of the debtor; a partnership in which the debtor is a general partner; a general partner of the debtor; or a relative of a general partner, director, officer, or person in control of the debtor.

Insider (of individual debtor)

Any relative of the debtor or of a general partner of the debtor; partnership inwhich the debtor is a general partner; general partner of the debtor; or corporation of which the debtor is a director, officer, or person in control.

Interrogatories

A form of discovery consisting of written questions to be answered in writing and under oath.

Issue

1. The disputed point between parties in a lawsuit; 2. To send out officially, as in a court issuing an order.

J

Joint administration

A court-approved mechanism under which two or more cases can be administered together. (Assuming no conflicts of interest, these separate businesses or individuals can pool their resources, hire the same professionals, etc.)

Joint petition

One bankruptcy petition filed by a husband and wife together.

Judge

An official of the Judicial branch with authority to decide lawsuits brought before courts. Used generically, the term judge may also refer to all judicial officers, including Supreme Court justices.

Judgeship

The position of judge. By statute, Congress authorizes the number of judgeships for each district and appellate court.

Judgment

The official decision of a court finally resolving the dispute between the parties to the lawsuit.

Judicial Conference of the United States

The policy-making entity for the federal court system. A 27-judge body whose presiding officer is the Chief Justice of the United States.

Jurisdiction

The legal authority of a court to hear and decide a certain type of case. It also is used as a synonym for venue, meaning the geographic area over which the court has territorial jurisdiction to decide cases.

Jurisprudence

The study of law and the structure of the legal system.

Jury

The group of persons selected to hear the evidence in a trial and render a verdict on matters of fact. See also grand jury.

Jury instructions

A judge's directions to the jury before it begins deliberations regarding the factual questions it must answer and the legal rules that it must apply.

L

Lawsuit

A legal action started by a plaintiff against a defendant based on a complaint that the defendant failed to perform a legal duty which resulted in harm to the plaintiff.

Lien

A charge on specific property that is designed to secure payment of a debt or performance of an obligation. A debtor may still be responsible for a lien after a discharge.

Litigation

A case, controversy, or lawsuit. Participants (plaintiffs and defendants) in lawsuits are called litigants.

Liquidation

The sale of a debtor's property with the proceeds to be used for the benefit of creditors.

Liquidated claim

A creditor's claim for a fixed amount of money.

M

Magistrate judge

A judicial officer of a district court who conducts initial proceedings in criminal cases, decides criminal misdemeanor cases, conducts many pretrial civil and criminal matters on behalf of district judges, and decides civil cases with the consent of the parties.

Means test

Section 707(b)(2) of the Bankruptcy Code applies a "means test" to determine whether an individual debtor's chapter 7 filing is presumed to be an abuse of the Bankruptcy Code requiring dismissal or conversion of the case (generally to chapter 13). Abuse is presumed if the debtor's aggregate current monthly income (see definition above) over 5 years, net of certain statutorily allowed expenses is more than (i) $10,000, or (ii) 25% of the debtor's nonpriority unsecured debt, as long as that amount is at least $6,000. The debtor may rebut a presumption of abuse only by a showing of special circumstances that justify additional expenses or adjustments of current monthly income.

Mental health treatment

Special condition the court imposes to require an individual to undergo evaluation and treatment for a mental disorder. Treatment may include psychiatric, psychological, and sex offense-specific evaluations, inpatient or outpatient counseling, and medication.

Misdemeanor

An offense punishable by one year of imprisonment or less. See also felony.

Mistrial

An invalid trial, caused by fundamental error. When a mistrial is declared, the trial must start again with the selection of a new jury.

Moot

Not subject to a court ruling because the controversy has not actually arisen, or has ended.

Motion

A request by a litigant to a judge for a decision on an issue relating to the case.

Motion to lift the automatic stay

A request by a creditor to allow the creditor to take action against the debtor or the debtor's property that would otherwise be prohibited by the automatic stay.

Motion in Limine

A pretrial motion requesting the court to prohibit the other side from presenting, or even referring to, evidence on matters said to be so highly prejudicial that no steps taken by the judge can prevent the jury from being unduly influenced.

N

No-asset case

A Chapter 7 case in which there are no assets available to satisfy any portion of the creditors' unsecured claims.

Nolo contendere

No contest. A plea of nolo contendere has the same effect as a plea of guilty, as far as the criminal sentence is concerned, but may not be considered as an admission of guilt for any other purpose.

Nondischargeable debt

A debt that cannot be eliminated in bankruptcy. Examples include a home mortgage, debts for alimony or child support, certain taxes, debts for most government funded or guaranteed educational loans or benefit overpayments, debts arising from death or personal injury caused by driving while intoxicated or under the influence of drugs, and debts for restitution or a criminal fine included in a sentence on the debtor's conviction of a crime. Some debts, such as debts for money or property obtained by false pretenses and debts for fraud or defalcation while acting in a fiduciary capacity may be declared nondischargeable only if a creditor timely files and prevails in a nondischargeability action.

Nonexempt assets

Property of a debtor that can be liquidated to satisfy claims of creditors.

O

Objection to dischargeability

A trustee's or creditor's objection to the debtor being released from personal liability for certain dischargeable debts. Common reasons include allegations that the debt to be discharged was incurred by false pretenses or that debt arose because of the debtor's fraud while acting as a fiduciary.

Objection to exemptions

A trustee's or creditor's objection to the debtor's attempt to claim certain property as exempt from liquidation by the trustee to creditors.

Opinion

A judge's written explanation of the decision of the court. Because a case may be heard by three or more judges in the court of appeals, the opinion in appellate decisions can take several forms. If all the judges completely agree on the result, one judge will write the opinion for all. If all the judges do not agree, the formal decision will be based upon the view of the majority, and one member of the majority will write the opinion. The judges who did not agree with the majority may write separately in dissenting or concurring opinions to present their views. A dissenting opinion disagrees with the majority opinion because of the reasoning and/or the principles of law the majority used to decide the case. A concurring opinion agrees with the decision of the majority opinion, but offers further comment or clarification or even an entirely different reason for reaching the same result. Only the majority opinion can serve as binding precedent in future cases. See also precedent.

Oral argument

An opportunity for lawyers to summarize their position before the court and also to answer the judges' questions.

P

Panel

1. In appellate cases, a group of judges (usually three) assigned to decide the case; 2. In the jury selection process, the group of potential jurors; 3. The list of attorneys who are both available and qualified to serve as court-appointed counsel for criminal defendants who cannot afford their own counsel.

Parole

The release of a prison inmate – granted by the U.S. Parole Commission – after the inmate has completed part of his or her sentence in a federal prison. When the parolee is released to the community, he or she is placed under the supervision of a U.S. probation officer.

The Sentencing Reform Act of 1984 abolished parole in favor of a determinate sentencing system in which the sentence is set by sentencing guidelines. Now, without the option of parole, the term of imprisonment the court imposes is the actual time the person spends in prison.

Party in interest

A party who has standing to be heard by the court in a matter to be decided in the bankruptcy case. The debtor, U.S. trustee or bankruptcy administrator, case trustee, and creditors are parties in interest for most matters.

Petition preparer

A business not authorized to practice law that prepares bankruptcy petitions.

Per curiam

Latin, meaning "for the court." In appellate courts, often refers to an unsigned opinion.

Peremptory challenge

A district court may grant each side in a civil or criminal trial the right to exclude a certain number of prospective jurors without cause or giving a reason.

Petit jury (or trial jury)

A group of citizens who hear the evidence presented by both sides at trial and determine the facts in dispute. Federal criminal juries consist of 12 persons. Federal civil juries consist of at least six persons.

Petition

The document that initiates the filing of a bankruptcy proceeding, setting forth basic information regarding the debtor, including name, address, chapter under which the case is filed, and estimated amount of assets and liabilities.

Petty offense

A federal misdemeanor punishable by six months or less in prison.

Plaintiff

A person or business that files a formal complaint with the court.

Plan

A debtor's detailed description of how the debtor proposes to pay creditors' claims over a fixed period of time.

Plea

In a criminal case, the defendant's statement pleading "guilty" or "not guilty" in answer to the charges. See also nolo contendere.

Pleadings

Written statements filed with the court that describe a party's legal or factual assertions about the case.

Postpetition transfer

A transfer of the debtor's property made after the commencement of the case.

Prebankruptcy planning

The arrangement (or rearrangement) of a debtor's property to allow the debtor to take maximum advantage of exemptions. (Prebankruptcy planning typically includes converting nonexempt assets into exempt assets.)

Precedent

A court decision in an earlier case with facts and legal issues similar to a dispute currently before a court. Judges will generally "follow precedent" - meaning that they use the principles established in earlier cases to decide new cases that have similar facts and raise similar legal issues. A judge will disregard precedent if a party can show that the earlier case was wrongly decided, or that it differed in some significant way from the current case.

Preferential debt payment

A debt payment made to a creditor in the 90-day period before a debtor files bankruptcy (or within one year if the creditor was an insider) that gives the creditor more than the creditor would receive in the debtor's chapter 7 case.

Presentence report

A report prepared by a court's probation officer, after a person has been convicted of an offense, summarizing for the court the background information needed to determine the appropriate sentence.

Pretrial conference

A meeting of the judge and lawyers to plan the trial, to discuss which matters should be presented to the jury, to review proposed evidence and witnesses, and to set a trial schedule. Typically, the judge and the parties also discuss the possibility of settlement of the case.

Pretrial services

A function of the federal courts that takes place at the very start of the criminal justice process – after a person has been arrested and charged with a federal crime and before he or she goes to trial. Pretrial services officers focus on investigating the backgrounds of these persons to help the court determine whether to release or detain them while they await trial. The decision is based on whether these individuals are likely to flee or pose a threat to the community. If the court orders release, a pretrial services officer supervises the person in the community until he or she returns to court.

Priority

The Bankruptcy Code's statutory ranking of unsecured claims that determines the order in which unsecured claims will be paid if there is not enough money to pay all unsecured claims in full.

Priority claim

An unsecured claim that is entitled to be paid ahead of other unsecured claims that are not entitled to priority status. Priority refers to the order in which these unsecured claims are to be paid.

Probation

Sentencing option in the federal courts. With probation, instead of sending an individual to prison, the court releases the person to the community and orders him or her to complete a period of supervision monitored by a U.S. probation officer and to abide by certain conditions.

Probation officer

Officers of the probation office of a court. Probation officer duties include conducting presentence investigations, preparing presentence reports on convicted defendants, and supervising released defendants.

Procedure

The rules for conducting a lawsuit; there are rules of civil procedure, criminal procedure, evidence, bankruptcy, and appellate procedure.

Proof of claim

A written statement describing the reason a debtor owes a creditor money, which typically sets forth the amount of money owed. (There is an official form for this purpose.)

Pro per

A slang expression sometimes used to refer to a pro se litigant. It is a corruption of the Latin phrase "in propria persona."

Property of the estate

All legal or equitable interests of the debtor in property as of the commencement of the case.

Pro se

Representing oneself. Serving as one's own lawyer.

Prosecute

To charge someone with a crime. A prosecutor tries a criminal case on behalf of the government.

Pro tem

Temporary.

R

Reaffirmation agreement

An agreement by a debtor to continue paying a dischargeable debt after the bankruptcy, usually for the purpose of keeping collateral or mortgaged property that would otherwise be subject to repossession.

Record

A written account of the proceedings in a case, including all pleadings, evidence, and exhibits submitted in the course of the case.

Redemption

A procedure in a Chapter 7 case whereby a debtor removes a secured creditor's lien on collateral by paying the creditor the value of the property. The debtor may then retain the property.

Remand

Send back.

Reverse

The act of a court setting aside the decision of a lower court. A reversal is often accompanied by a remand to the lower court for further proceedings.

S

Sanction

A penalty or other type of enforcement used to bring about compliance with the law or with rules and regulations.

Schedules

Lists submitted by the debtor along with the petition (or shortly thereafter) showing the debtor's assets, liabilities, and other financial information. (There are official forms a debtor must use.)

Secured creditor

A secured creditor is an individual or business that holds a claim against the debtor that is secured by a lien on property of the estate. The property subject to the lien is the secured creditor's collateral.

Secured debt

Debt backed by a mortgage, pledge of collateral, or other lien; debt for which the creditor has the right to pursue specific pledged property upon default. Examples include home mortgages, auto loans and tax liens.

Senior judge

A federal judge who, after attaining the requisite age and length of judicial experience, takes senior status, thus creating a vacancy among a court's active judges. A senior judge retains the judicial office and may cut back his or her workload by as much as 75 percent, but many opt to keep a larger caseload.

Sentence

The punishment ordered by a court for a defendant convicted of a crime.

Sentencing guidelines

A set of rules and principles established by the United States Sentencing Commission that trial judges use to determine the sentence for a convicted defendant.

Service of process

The delivery of writs or summonses to the appropriate party.

Settlement

Parties to a lawsuit resolve their dispute without having a trial. Settlements often involve the payment of compensation by one party in at least partial satisfaction of the other party's claims, but usually do not include the admission of fault.

Sequester

To separate. Sometimes juries are sequestered from outside influences during their deliberations.

Small business case

A special type of chapter 11 case in which there is no creditors' committee (or the creditors' committee is deemed inactive by the court) and in which the debtor is subject to more oversight by the U.S. trustee than other chapter 11 debtors. The Bankruptcy Code contains certain provisions designed to reduce the time a small business debtor is in bankruptcy.

Statement of financial affairs

A series of questions the debtor must answer in writing concerning sources of income, transfers of property, lawsuits by creditors, etc. (There is an official form a debtor must use.)

Statement of intention

A declaration made by a chapter 7 debtor concerning plans for dealing with consumer debts that are secured by property of the estate.

Standard of proof

Degree of proof required. In criminal cases, prosecutors must prove a defendant's guilt "beyond a reasonable doubt." The majority of civil lawsuits require proof "by a preponderance of the evidence" (50 percent plus), but in some the standard is higher and requires "clear and convincing" proof.

Statute

A law passed by a legislature.

Statute of limitations

The time within which a lawsuit must be filed or a criminal prosecution begun. The deadline can vary, depending on the type of civil case or the crime charged.

Sua sponte

Latin, meaning "of its own will." Often refers to a court taking an action in a case without being asked to do so by either side.

Subordination

The act or process by which a person's rights or claims are ranked below those of others.

Subpoena

A command, issued under a court's authority, to a witness to appear and give testimony.

Subpoena duces tecum

A command to a witness to appear and produce documents.

Substance abuse treatment

A special condition the court imposes that requires an individual to undergo testing and treatment for abuse of illegal drugs, prescription drugs, or alcohol. Treatment may include inpatient or outpatient counseling and detoxification.

Substantial abuse

The characterization of a bankruptcy case filed by an individual whose debts are primarily consumer debts where the court finds that the granting of relief would be an abuse of chapter 7 because, for example, the debtor can pay its debts.

Substantive consolidation

Putting the assets and liabilities of two or more related debtors into a single pool to pay creditors. (Courts are reluctant to allow substantive consolidation since the action must not only justify the benefit that one set of creditors receives, but also the harm that other creditors suffer as a result.)

Summary judgment

A decision made on the basis of statements and evidence presented for the record without a trial. It is used when it is not necessary to resolve any factual disputes in the case. Summary judgment is granted when – on the undisputed facts in the record – one party is entitled to judgment as a matter of law.

Supervised release

Term of supervision served after a person is released from prison. The court imposes supervised release during sentencing in addition to the sentence of imprisonment. Unlike parole, supervised release does not replace a portion of the sentence of imprisonment but is in addition to the time spent in prison. U.S. probation officers supervise people on supervised release.

T

Temporary restraining order

Akin to a preliminary injunction, it is a judge's short-term order forbidding certain actions until a full hearing can be conducted. Often referred to as a TRO.

Testimony

Evidence presented orally by witnesses during trials or before grand juries.

Toll

See statute of limitations.

Tort

A civil, not criminal, wrong. A negligent or intentional injury against a person or property, with the exception of breach of contract.

Transfer

Any mode or means by which a debtor disposes of or parts with his/her property.

Transcript

A written, word-for-word record of what was said, either in a proceeding such as a trial, or during some other formal conversation, such as a hearing or oral deposition.

Trustee

The representative of the bankruptcy estate who exercises statutory powers, principally for the benefit of the unsecured creditors, under the general supervision of the court and the direct supervision of the U.S. trustee or bankruptcy administrator. The trustee is a private individual or corporation appointed in all chapter 7, chapter 12, and chapter 13 cases and some chapter 11 cases. The trustee's responsibilities include reviewing the debtor's petition and schedules and bringing actions against creditors or the debtor to recover property of the bankruptcy estate. In chapter 7, the trustee liquidates property of the estate, and makes distributions to creditors. Trustees in chapter 12 and 13 have similar duties to a chapter 7 trustee and the additional responsibilities of overseeing the debtor's plan, receiving payments from debtors, and disbursing plan payments to creditors.

Typing service

A business not authorized to practice law that prepares bankruptcy petitions.

U

U.S. attorney

A lawyer appointed by the President in each judicial district to prosecute and defend cases for the federal government. The U.S. Attorney employs a staff of Assistant U.S. Attorneys who appear as the government's attorneys in individual cases.

U.S. trustee

An officer of the U.S. Department of Justice responsible for supervising the administration of bankruptcy cases, estates, and trustees; monitoring plans and disclosure statements; monitoring creditors' committees; monitoring fee applications; and performing other statutory duties.

Undersecured claim

A debt secured by property that is worth less than the amount of the debt.

Undue hardship

The most widely used test for evaluating undue hardship in the dischargeability of a student loan includes three conditions: (1) the debtor cannot maintain –

based on current income and expenses – a minimal standard of living if forced to repay the loans; (2) there are indications that the state of affairs is likely to persist for a significant portion of the repayment period; and (3) the debtor made good faith efforts to repay the loans.

Unlawful detainer action

A lawsuit brought by a landlord against a tenant to evict the tenant from rental property – usually for nonpayment of rent.

Unliquidated claim

A claim for which a specific value has not been determined.

Unscheduled debt

A debt that should have been listed by the debtor in the schedules filed with the court but was not. (Depending on the circumstances, an unscheduled debt may or may not be discharged.)

Unsecured claim

A claim or debt for which a creditor holds no special assurance of payment, such as a mortgage or lien; a debt for which credit was extended based solely upon the creditor's assessment of the debtor's future ability to pay.

Uphold

The appellate court agrees with the lower court decision and allows it to stand. See affirmed.

V

Venue

The geographic area in which a court has jurisdiction. A change of venue is a change or transfer of a case from one judicial district to another.

Verdict

The decision of a trial jury or a judge that determines the guilt or innocence of a criminal defendant, or that determines the final outcome of a civil case.

Voir dire

Jury selection process of questioning prospective jurors, to ascertain their qualifications and determine any basis for challenge.

Voluntary transfer

A transfer of a debtor's property with the debtor's consent.

W

Wage garnishment

A nonbankruptcy legal proceeding whereby a plaintiff or creditor seeks to subject to his or her claim the future wages of a debtor. In other words, the creditor seeks to have part of the debtor's future wages paid to the creditor for a debt owed to the creditor.

Warrant

Court authorization, most often for law enforcement officers, to conduct a search or make an arrest.

Witness

A person called upon by either side in a lawsuit to give testimony before the court or jury.

Writ

A written court order directing a person to take, or refrain from taking, a certain act.

Writ of certiorari

An order issued by the U.S. Supreme Court directing the lower court to transmit records for a case which it will hear on appeal.